Praise for Alicia Partnoy's Th
Tales of Disappearance & Surv

"Lyrical, ebullient, charming, vigorous and ingenious..."
— San Francisco Chronicle

"Alicia Partnoy's accounts are courageous, understated, chilling; and they are very well written."
— Bobbie Ann Mason

"Remarkable... for her flinty humor and her determination to take joy from any source — the smell of rain, the imagined taste of a soft drink, the sight of her own feet through a loosely tied blindfold."
–Tobias Wolff

"Strength and courage... is well portrayed..."
—The Nation

"A testimony to the healing powers of art and imagination, of humor and compassion..."
—The Guardian

"The common thread of Partnoy's tales is a message of love for humanity..."
— Cleveland Plain Dealer

"Partnoy's triumph is to have discovered under her blindfold another pair of eyes, eyes that found a reason to survive in a world that did not deserve her. It is our privilege to look through those eyes for a short time, and to be reminded that we who claim freedom as our birthright must raise our voices, again and again, on behalf of those imprisoned in all the Little Schools around the world."
— Pittsburgh Post-Gazette

"Partnoy's spirit of resistance is also a spirit of creativity and hope ."
– In These Times

Revenge of the Apple

Venganza de la manzana

Alicia Partnoy

Translated by
Richard Schaaf, Regina Kreger, and Alicia Partnoy

Illustrated by Raquel Partnoy

CLEIS
PRESS

Published in the United States by Cleis Press Inc., P.O. Box 8933, Pittsburgh, Pennsylvania 15221, and P.O. Box 14684, San Francisco, California 94114.

Printed in the United States.
Printed on acid-free paper.
Cover design: Pete Ivey
Cover art: Raquel Partnoy
Typesetting: CaliCo Graphics
Logo art: Juana Alicia

First Edition.
10 9 8 7 6 5 4 3 2 1

Library of Congress Cataloging-in-Publication Data

Partnoy, Alicia, 1955-
    Revenge of the apple = Venganza de la manzana / by Alicia Partnoy; translated by Richard Schaaf, Regina Kreger, and Alicia Partnoy ; illustrated by Raquel Partnoy. — 1st ed.
        p. cm.
    ISBN: 0-939416-62-X (cloth) : $24.95. — ISBN: 0-939416-63-8 (pbk.): $8.95
    I. Title. II. Title: Venganza de la manzana.
PQ7079.2.P37R48   1992
861 — dc20   92-2417
                                                                      CIP

to my parents
a mis padres

Special thanks to Olga Madruga, Lisa Wheaton and Sandra Wheaton for the translation of previous versions of some of these poems.

Indice/Contents

III. La muerte, mi vecina/Death, My Neighbor

IV. Testimonios/Testimonies

Raquel Partnoy
92

Introduction

In a prison cell in South America, a woman is trying to remember every single poem she has ever written. Her memory leaps thirteen years to fish out her first poem, written when she was nine: three stanzas in celebration of Spring and the rebirth of nature.

The woman is a "disappeared." No one, except for the military authorities who kidnaped her from her home, knows her whereabouts. The year is 1977. The country, Argentina.

The prisoner of our story has been transferred to a new location with new rules. Her wrists no longer bound, she is now "free" to dance around this nine-by-six cell, to wash her hands and to enjoy the "privilege" of her own toilet. No longer blindfolded, she is now "free" to read the hundreds of messages scratched into the walls with the bottom edges of toothpaste tubes. Most importantly, her captors have given her a precious pen and a brand new notebook.

Our prisoner does not write new poems. It would hurt her immensely to search for words to describe the past three and a half months of her life in a concentration camp where torture, executions, sexual harassment, hunger, and the certainty of an imminent death haunt the victims. How could she bear, in the solitude of this cell, to write about the loss of her closest friends, killed by the military after months of torment in that secret detention place? Where could she find the spiritual strength to write about her eighteen-month-old daughter, left behind, and whom the torturers insisted they were going to kill? What words could express the horror of knowing that a baby born in that place, cynically called the Little School, was "adopted" by one of his mother's torturers?

She chooses, then, not to write new poems. Instead, she makes a long list: the titles of all the poems she has written since childhood. Every day she tries to remember and record them in her notebook. Every night she fears for the arrival of the jailers. They will inject her with an anesthetic and, once she is unconscious, kill her in a faked "confrontation" with the Army. Or they will let her go, only to shoot her in the back. Or drop her from a helicopter into the Atlantic Ocean, a few miles away from her hometown of Bahía Blanca.

She does not know why she still fears the worst at night. It was noon, after all, when they arrested her. Daylight was never a deterrence for the thousands of kidnapings and murders conducted by the military since the coup of March 1976.

The woman writes in her notebook for fifty-two days. The day she records the last poem she can remember, the authorities notify her that she is no longer a "disappeared." As a political prisoner, she is allowed to see her family and small daughter, who has miraculously survived because the military left her with neighbors rather than kidnap her along with her mother. The neighbors then called the woman's parents who came for the child. Later the poet will learn that more than four hundred children were not as "lucky" as hers. Born in captivity or taken away by the authorities, many children ended up separated from their families and sometimes placed in the homes of those responsible for their tragedies.

She has recovered her child and her poetry. Many years later the woman will come to the realization that the recovery of her old poems in that notebook amounted to the recovery of her soul, her history. While it will take her a long time to understand the ways her poetry helped her survive, it will only take her a few days to find out that under a repressive regime, poetry can be terribly dangerous.

On the first visit with her husband, she learns that during torture sessions, he was interrogated about a poem she had written, a poem the military had found in the couple's home. The interrogators insisted that the lines "he died because he was/too much light and too much song" were dedicated to one of the victims of their repression, and not to a creek in a park close to the couple's house. The creek had been channeled underground and all its beauty had been lost. The torturers demanded the name of the "person" for whom the poem had been written. That poem, like the woman and her husband, was a hostage of the military regime. So were the prisoner's family: her small daughter whose world was destroyed in barely half an hour one hot January day; her parents, who desperately searched for her while trying to cope with the unbearable pain of her disappearance; her younger brother, who tried to entertain, distract the little girl while hiding the rage, the impotence, the deep fear that would soon trigger the mental illness that led to his suicide.

In October of 1977, ten long months after her capture, the woman is transferred to a prison for political prisoners in Buenos Aires. There, the inmates are allowed to leave their crammed cells for three hours each day. Indoor recess is a time for writing workshops, news analysis, mothers' groups, first aid courses, political meetings, dance classes, gymnastics and, of course, theatre performances and poetry readings. None of these activities is allowed by prison authorities. If caught, the participants are subject to punishment: no visits, no recess, no correspondence, no books and, in the worst of cases, complete isolation in a bare cell. Therefore, most of the performances are staged in the showers, a large area whose location at the end of a long corridor gives artists and audience the necessary time to flee or jump under the water when the guards approach. It is in the prison showers that the woman of this story first recites her own poetry. She encounters then what years later she will call "a truly captive audience."

Poetry is also collected in the prisoners' notebooks and in a literary "magazine" consisting of a few notebook pages, folded and bound with precious thread from colorful towels. Every few weeks, and sometimes as often as every few days, the prison authorities call for an inspection. Female guards strip search the prisoners and destroy everything in their cells, allegedly looking for contraband. They confiscate unfinished crafts; crochet and knitting needles fashioned from the plastic ends of toothbrushes; "candy" (political messages written in tiny letters and sealed in plastic wrapping); pain killers and alcoholic beverages distilled from fermented orange peels; and the poetry magazine. They also take books, notebooks and sweaters and pants they like for themselves.

Poems are seldom allowed to leave the jail. On special occasions the prisoners are permitted to mail poetry to their families. Always trying to stretch the limits, the woman risks sending poems on ordinary days. Sometimes she gets away with it. Once, the prisoner of our tale sends a letter home, enclosing a poem, "To My Daughter, Letter from Prison." That page comes back stamped "Censored: Marxist Contents." Obviously, a reference to the need to fight "for the happiness/of those who are our brothers our sisters" is considered such a dangerous statement that it has to be labeled Marxist. "So be it," says the prisoner. She has never read a single line by Marx in her entire life.

The censorship increases this woman's popularity as a prison poet. More and more often, she is called upon to write for the occasion, something she has always shied away from. She writes poems to be given as birthday presents and tokens of solidarity in bitter moments; she produces poetry to be performed on holidays. Her writings to her child must be fit to be sent to any prisoner's child. She does not know yet that she will have to defend these poems once she leaves the jail. Then she will have to "explain" her verses, something most poets dread. In this way her poetry, too tied to the situation that generated it, will finally regain its original strength when used as a tool to denounce injustice. But the woman of our tale is not concerned with these problems yet, for she does not know when or if she will be released. Meanwhile, poetry helps her survive, helps her lift the spirits of her friends.

On a bright December morning in 1979, the woman is transferred from jail to an airport. She has been expelled from her country. After briefly meeting family and friends, she takes her child's hand and boards the plane that will bring her to the United States.

Once in exile, she feels the pressing need to tell her story, to let everyone know how many were left behind in an Argentina swept by state terrorism. She also needs to tell people that they must do something so their nation, the United States of America, stops fostering dictatorships in Latin America.

The woman dives into her memory, searching for the English she studied for almost ten years. She refuses to pick up a dictionary, a sign of her deep conflict with the language of the land she did not choose as home. Her drive to tell makes her translate her experiences into testimony, essay, song, theater, short story. Poetry is her last refuge, the only place where her bitterness and rage blossom.

From the dismembered reality of exile, she, a poet, grasps an image that better defines herself: She will be a bridge. Extended between cultures, between experiences, she will help other Latin American women reach this shore with their own stories. "Maybe instead of bridges, we must be tunnels," suggests a friend, "carving deep into the foundations of this society, sending shock waves to the surface." Sometimes the poet wishes she really could be a tunnel.

She returns to Argentina in 1984 to appear before the Commission for the Investigation of Disappearances. Three years later she learns her testimony has been dismissed because the witnesses to her kidnaping were too frightened to speak up. Eventually they did testify, but by then a new law exempted from prosecution all but those who had committed atrocities under "extreme and aberrant circumstances." Those who acted under orders—nearly all in the armed forces—were spared trials.

In the United States, the woman knows she must understand her audience for her message to be effective. She learns that when people eagerly demand the details of her torture, they may be trying to protect themselves: the more horrendous the experience, the more removed from everyday life. Something so alien to their humanity can never really happen to them. "It's good that those things don't happen here," says a newspaper interviewer, or someone in an audience, looking for safety, for relief after listening to the horror of her story.

She struggles to find the words to tell them that many of those horrors occur because of the policies of their "safe" nation. She also learns that people can't relate to the other stories she wants to tell until they hear hers. By now, the woman is tired of speaking of herself. She finds a device: She tells her own tale in the third person.

Yes, I am the woman of this story. I was the rotten fruit, repressed by the military because I was just not going to accept the rule of dictators.

Let my juices ferment and join those of other troublemakers. Let us become the cider that inebriates the torturers to the point of nausea. We will be the refreshing, sparkling drink that the poor in my country, those who cannot afford champagne, pour in their glasses to celebrate life and the New Year.

Ours will be the revenge of the apple.

My revenge is to survive to tell the story. As a refugee who has settled in a "barrio" and an author who travels extensively, I have been shocked by the many contrasts this society offers. My daughter tells me of youngsters at her high school who die, victims of a violence that could be controlled in a fair, drug-free society. She once said, "It's true that you also have lost friends at a very young age, but they died for a cause ... These kids die for nothing." On the other hand, I sometimes visit the university campuses of the highly privileged and find the best-intentioned youngsters astonished to hear about the tragedies of our peoples. Many of them have not even heard of last year's riots in my Washington D.C. neighborhood.

Strange, almost surreal things have happened to me these past thirteen years. One morning I found myself doing my laundry in a dirty, overcrowded laundromat; that afternoon, I was approaching a mike at the Carter Presidential Center in Atlanta to address a symposium of former heads of state. One day at work I was dutifully answering phones when I received a call from home saying that my brother, my playmate, the illustrator of my childhood poems, had just shot himself in the head ... and the military authorities would not allow me to attend his funeral. I have had barely enough money to eat one month and the following month found myself flying to England, a best-selling author interviewed on the most important BBC shows of the week. I have breast-fed my little Eva Victoria, born of my exile in the United States, in the middle of my colonial literature class.

However, the oddest of all my experiences has been to learn so much about my Latin America, to meet so many people from my continent, while living in the city where the destruction of our homelife has so often been plotted. In this Washington D.C. I have been lucky to befriend Verónica de Negri from Chile, América Sosa and Claribel Alegría from El Salvador, Adriana Angel, a Colombian, her bags filled with pictures and stories from Nicaragua ... I have met Rigoberta Menchú and Julia Esquivel from Guatemala, Esmeralda Brown from Panama. I have learned about Domitila Barrios, survivor of a massacre in her Bolivia, Aridna Ojeda writing from jail in her Chile, María Tila Uribe collecting prison memoirs in her Colombia ... And, here, I have met Rene Epelbaum, María Isabel de Mariani, Hebe de Bonafini, Estela Carlotto, Chela Mignone, founders of the Mothers and Grandmothers of the Plaza de Mayo, a never-ending source of inspiration. In this city I have heard from Latin American refugees countless stories of repression, suffering and resistance.

When I travel and when I teach literature, all of them go with me. Their voices, like mine, gather the voices of their peoples. They, like me, are the fruits tossed out of their crates. Ours is the revenge of the apple: to come back after years of fermentation, our cider mixed with that of other survivors, to overpower with our sweetness the strength of the executioner who has cast us away, as rotten fruits, condemned to die in isolation.

Alicia Partnoy
Washington D.C.
July 1992

17

Datos biográficos

Me sacaron la tierra
de debajo
— a eso llaman destierro —
o sea que, de pronto,
me faltó el suelo
y me sobró distancia.

Pero un día,
antes de aquello,
me habían arrancado
la libertad de cuajo,
y entonces,
cuando me faltaba el aire
y me sobraban rejas,
me sentía
un poco mejor que antes,
que cuando me quitaron
a mi hija de los brazos:
en ese entonces
me faltaba todo — el futuro —
(podría decir que me sobró la vida).

Y sin embargo
todavía me acordaba
del día en que los milicos
metieron a mi patria entre barrotes,
ese día me sobró la fuerza
y me faltó el miedo.

Allí empezó la cosa.

Biographical Data

They booted my homeland
out from under me
— what they call exile —
that is, all of a sudden
the ground was gone
and distance lay everywhere before me.

But one day,
before that happened,
they stripped me
of my freedom,
and then —
gasping for air,
surrounded by iron bars —
I felt
a little better than when
they grabbed
my daughter out of my arms:
on that day,
everything — the future — was gone
(you could say I had too much of my own life).

And yet,
I still remembered the day the military
put my homeland behind bars:
on that day I had too much courage
and the fear was gone.

That's where it all began.

I.

Prison Poems
Poemas de la cárcel

1977-1979

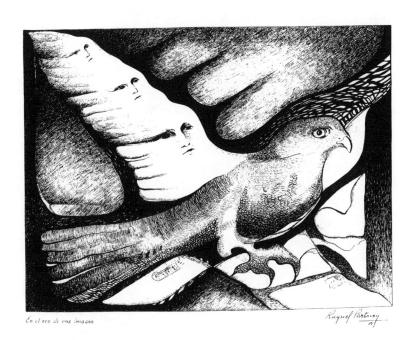

En el eco de una imagen

Raquel Partnoy

A mi hija
(Cartas desde la cárcel)

I.

Escuchá:
Mi garganta se hace amiga del viento
para llegar hasta vos
corazón tierno, ojos nuevos.
Escuchá:
Poné tu oído en el hueco de un caracol
o en el parlante infame
y escuchá.

La razón es tan simple
y tan sencilla
como la gota de agua
o la semilla
que te cabe en la palma de la mano.
La razón es bien simple:
No podía
dejar de pelear por la alegría
de aquellos que son nuestros hermanos.

II.

Para escribirte a vos
caramelo de sol, chiquita mía,
tendría . . .
tendría que juntar tanta ternura . . .
Y tu madre, mi amor,
tu madre es dura,
tiene de piedra el alma,
casi no llora nunca . . .
salvo para escribirte,
caramelo de sol,
cristalito de luna.

22

To My Daughter
(Letters from Prison)

I.

Listen:
My throat befriends the winds
to reach you
dear gentle heart, new eyes.
Listen:
place your ear to a sea shell,
or to this infamous prison phone,
and listen.

The reason is so simple,
so pure,
like a drop of water
or a seed
that fits in the palm of your hand.
The reason is so very simple:
I could not
keep from fighting for the happiness
of those who are our brothers our sisters.

II.

To write you,
my sun caramel, my *chiquita*,
I would have to . . .
I would have to gather so much tenderness . . .
And your mother, my love,
your mother has hardened,
her soul is made of stone,
she almost never cries . . .
except when she writes to you,
my sun caramel,
my moon crystal.

III.

Hoy suelto las amarras
que aprisionan mis sueños
y llego hasta tu orilla
doradita de sol.
Niña soy navegante
de un barco de ilusiones
con un único puerto:
tu carita y tu voz.
Abrocharte el zapato,
desatarte la risa,
caminar a tu lado
por un mundo mejor.
Para esas tareas
sé que está haciendo falta
mi mano y mi ternura,
mi libertad y mi voz.
Desatarte la risa,
abrocharte el zapato,
destruir las murallas
que nos tapan el sol . . .
Para esas tareas
es que estoy preparando
mi palabra y mi vida,
mi puño y mi
      canción.

III.

Today I cast off the lines
imprisoning my dreams
and I arrive at your golden
sun-drenched shore.
My dear daughter, I am a sailor
on a ship of hopeful dreams
with one port of call:
your soft face and your voice.
To buckle your shoes,
to let loose your laughter,
to walk by your side
through a better world . . .
For these tasks
I know what is needed:
my hands and my tenderness,
my freedom and my voice.
To let loose your laughter,
to buckle your shoes,
to tear down the walls
that block out the sun . . .
It is for these tasks
I am preparing
my word, my life,
my fist and my
    song.

Visita

Mamá rompe los viernes
cerrojos y candados
para darte una ronda
de minutos contados.
Papá, desde bien lejos,
— su día amurallado —,
sueña con tu piel tibia
y tus minutos contados.
Si yo pudiera, niña,
explicarte el por qué
de todos los cerrojos,
de tódos los candados,
de todos los barrotes,
de las altas murallas,
de todos pero todos
los minutos contados . . .
Niña si yo pudiera
devorar el espacio
para hacer una ronda
lejos de tanta cárcel . . .
ronda libre
y mis manos
sin minutos contados . . .

Visit

On Fridays Mama breaks through
the locks and gates
to play ring-around-the-rosy with you,
counting the minutes.
Papa, from far away
in his walled-in day,
dreams of your warm skin
and your numbered minutes.
If I could, dear child,
explain to you the reason
for all the locks,
for all the gates,
for all the bars,
for the high walls,
for all ... all
the numbered minutes ...
My child, if I could
devour space
and play ring-around-the-rosy
far from every prison ...
oh we'd be playing free
and my hands
would lose all track of time ...

Doña Serpiente

Qué va a hacer Doña Serpiente
cuando vea de repente
que el árbol que ha talado
reproduce simiente?
Cuando la rama cortada
crezca de nuevo hacia el cielo,
cuando el ala mutilada
vuelva a remontar el vuelo,
cuando se nos vuelvan canto
el llanto y el desconsuelo?
Qué va a hacer Doña Serpiente
cuando, a fuerza de pelearlo,
todo sea diferente?

Juego

Qué rabiosa está la luna
que entra por la ventana
metiéndoseme en los ojos
quiere enlunarme hasta el alma.
La luna, desde allí afuera,
mira dentro de esta jaula.
de alambre tejido y rejas.
Ella presa, que esperanza!

La luna, desde allí afuera
mira dentro de esta jaula.

Doña Snake

What will you do, Doña Snake,
when suddenly you see
that the felled tree
reproduces new seeds?
When the severed branch
grows anew toward the sky,
when the mutilated wing
once again soars,
when our tears our affliction
turn to song?
What will you do, Doña Snake,
when, through our struggling,
everything is different?

A Game

How rabid this moon
that filters through the window,
flooding my eyes,
seeking to bathe my very soul in moonlight.
From here, inside, the moon
is the one in the cell
of cage wire and iron bars.
She, a prisoner. Imagine!

From there, outside, the moon
looks right into this cell.

A un amigo cristiano
asesinado por los militares

... Y derramó su luz
la herida del costado.
... Y floreció en rubíes
su cuerpo atormentado.
Su grito persistió.
Su grito fue un llamado.
El no murió en la cruz,
él muere cada día.
El no murió en la cruz,
él vive en la alegría.
Hermano de la luz,
sueños crucificados,
tu grito persistió
— tu grito y tu llamado —.
Hermano de la luz,
árbol despedazado,
el surco que labraste ...
pronto será sembrado!

For a Christian Friend
Assassinated by the Military

... And his light poured
from the wound in his side.
...And rubies blossomed
from his tortured body.
His cry persisted.
His cry was a call.
He did not die on the cross,
he dies every day.
He did not die on the cross,
he lives in our joy.
Brother of light,
crucified dreams,
your cry persisted
— your cry and your call —.
Brother of light,
fallen tree,
the furrow you plow . . .
will soon be sown!

II.

Love and Other Places
El amor y otros lugares

Mi madero y yo

I.

Este hombre al que llamo compañero
es un trozo de mi barca,
es un madero
que me salva de hundirme
hasta los huesos
en el mar implacable del exilio.

II.

Y yo que no creía en los naufragios,
en las absurdas historias
de las quillas
destrozadas contra costas inmutables,
en los trozos de barco
a la deriva
y en el sobreviviente que — infaltable —
abrazado a un madero
salvaba alma y pellejo . . .
Ahora mirame:
Náufraga de mi tierra,
entre tus brazos,
quiero salvarme entera
hasta la costa.

III.

Después de los naufragios
siempre quedan

My Lifeboard and I

I.

This man whom I call *compañero*
is part of my boat,
he is my lifeboard
that keeps me from sinking
down to my bones
in the implacable sea of exile.

II.

And I who never believed in shipwrecks,
in ridiculous stories
of hulls
shattered against immutable coasts,
in pieces of boats
adrift,
and in the survivor who — not to be missed —
embraced his lifeboard
and saved his soul and his skin . . .
Now look at me:
Shipwrecked from my homeland,
wrapped in your arms,
I want to remain whole,
I want to reach my coast.

III.

After shipwrecks
pieces of wood

en la playa
pedazos de madera
y en tierra firme
los sobrevivientes.
Yo quisiera, mi amor,
que mi madero
fuera pilar de mi casa
en tierra firme
o en tierra libre:
en mi patria
   y con mi gente.

are always left
on the sand,
and survivors
on firm land.
Oh how I wish, my love,
that my lifeboard
were a pillar of my homeland
on firm land
or in a free land:
in my homeland
   with my people.

Carta

Desde mi territorio de exilios, desde donde
es un puente el lenguaje, te escribo ...

Caracolea mi alma
en un papel
en letras retorcidas
de calor.
Revolotea mi alma
en un papel
en la boca insaciable del buzon.
Te estoy mandando mi alma
en un papel.

Te escribo.
Con el papel me voy.

This Letter

From my territory of exiles, where language
is a bridge, I am writing to you . . .

My soul caracoles
on this piece of paper,
the letters writhing
in the heat.
My soul flutters its wings
on this piece of paper,
flies into the mailbox's insatiable mouth.
On this piece of paper
I am sending you my soul.

I am writing to you.
With this piece of paper, I am going.

Instantánea

No huele a flores la Plaza
de las Palomas, huele a vino,
a latas de cerveza.
Si andás desprevenido te sorprende
el tufo desparejo
de la miseria.

Al borde de la tarde
el camión de la sopa organiza
una fila obediente y resignada.
Este es el corazón
del barrio latino en Adams Morgan.

Apenas a unas cuadras
está la Casa Blanca.

. . . si yo no lloro . . .

. . . si yo no lloro, no,
no estoy llorando.
Es sólo un grito de agua
que se escapa
por entre las fisuras
de mi cuerpo . . .

Snapshot

It doesn't smell like a plaza full of flowers.
Pigeon Park smells of wine,
beer cans.
If you just happen to be walking by there,
the squalid stench of misery
hits you.

On the edge of dusk
the soup truck organizes
an obedient and resigned line.
This is the heart
of the *barrio* in Adams Morgan.

Just a few blocks away
is the White House.

... no, I do not cry ...

... no, I do not cry, no,
I'm not crying.
It's just the tears
screaming,
escaping
through the cracks
in my body ...

Lealtad

Como cuchillo de agua
la lealtad
te limpia y te despena.
Te deja
un solo camino en línea recta.

Lindo es doblar esquinas!

La lealtad,
ese miedo
de encontrarse a sí mismo
al dar la vuelta.

Comunicación

Yo te hablo de poesía
y vos me preguntás
a qué hora comemos.
Lo peor es que
yo también tengo hambre.

Loyalty

Loyalty
like a knife pure as water,
cleans you, puts you out of your misery.
It leaves you
on one long and straight road.

How wonderful to turn corners!

Loyalty
that fear of finding
yourself
around the corner.

Communication

I am talking to you about poetry
and you say
when do we eat.
The worst of it is
I'm hungry too.

Amor de entrecasa

Porque este amor modesto y de entrecasa
— así como lo ven, sencillo, sin adornos —
es el que nos mantiene con los pies en la tierra,
es el que engendra frutos de nuestro inconformismo,
y nos tira un madero en mitad del naufragio.
De vez en cuando enciende miles de lucecitas
y se pone la ropa de salir y destapa
botellas de burbujas y cajitas de risa.
Es que, de vez en cuando, cuando cuadra el momento,
recuerda, él también, que es un sobreviviente.

Sobreviviente

Llevo mi rabia como un pez muerto,
fláccido y maloliente entre los brazos.
La aprieto contra el pecho,
le susurro,
la gente me huye en los caminos . . .
No sé si es el olor a muerte
o es el miedo
de que el calor de mi cuerpo
la reanime.

A Homespun Love

Because this humble and homespun love
— just as you see it, simple, unadorned —
is what keeps our feet on the ground,
is what engenders the fruit of our nonconformity,
and throws us a lifeboard amidst the shipwreck.
Every so often our love blazes like thousands of stars,
gets dressed up to go out and uncorks
bottles of effervescence, cases of laughter.
You see, every so often, when the moment is right,
our love recalls that it is, like we are, a survivor.

Survivor

I carry my rage like a dead fish,
limp and stinking in my arms.
I press it against my breast,
whisper to it,
people on the streets flee from me ...
I don't know: is it the smell of death
that makes them flee
or is it the fear
that my body's warmth
might bring rage back to life?

De exilio y amargura

Quiero comerme el sol a gajos esta tarde,
y reventar en el aire mi pasado;
quiero reir hasta el fondo de mis huesos,
y sacudirme cadenas con la risa.

Pero recuerdo a mi gente que pelea
y se sacude cadenas con las ganas
de comerse de una vez el sol a gajos
y despertarse al aire del futuro.

Yo, náufraga de exilio y sin tibiezas,
deliro lejos del sol y de mi gente.

Exile and Bitterness

This afternoon I want to feast on slices of sunlight
and blow away my past into the air;
I want to laugh so hard my bones hurt,
and shake off my chains with the laughter.

But I remember my people fighting back,
shaking off their chains with the same desire
to devour without let-up slices of sunlight
and wake up breathing the air of the future.

I, shipwrecked by exile and without warmth,
rave delirious far from the sun and my people.

A Ruth

I.

Tu sueño era el nombre
de todos nuestros sueños.
Construímos trincheras
contra las pesadillas.
Pero no fué bastante.
Anidaba lo amargo
trenzado en las raíces
de tu árbol de futuro.
Se apagó el mediodía.
Fué hora de las nubes.

II.

Pequeño cataclismo.
Huracán de entrecasa.
Te cambiaron el sitio
de los juguetes, la altura
de la cama, los rostros
del amor, el techo ...
Entonces, siempre entonces,
se transformaba todo,
todo, menos tu miedo.
Brotarían las sombras.

To Ruth

I.

Your dream was the name
of all our dreams.
We dug trenches
against the nightmares.
But it was not enough.
Entwined among the roots
of your future tree,
bitterness built its nest.
The noonday sun died out.
It was a time of dark clouds.

II.

A cataclysmic tremor,
a homespun hurricane,
changed where you kept
your toys, the height
of your bed, the faces
of love, the roof tiles. . .
Then—always back then—
everything was transformed,
everything but your fear.
The shadows would come.

A mi viejo

A fuerza de tanta muerte y tanto invierno
se nos va desgastando la corteza,
se nos aprietan los nudos de las vetas,
nos brotan cicatrices en las ramas
y hasta nos pesan los nidos en la copa.

Sin embargo no nos damos por vencidos
en tanto haya quien cuente con nuestra sombra.

To My Father

So much death and so many winters
have eaten away at our bark,
knots tighten their grip on our lifelines,
scars blossom on our branches,
and even the birds' nests weigh down our crowns.

Still, we never give ourselves up for defeated
while there is one person who needs our shade.

III.

Death, My Neighbor
La muerte, mi vecina

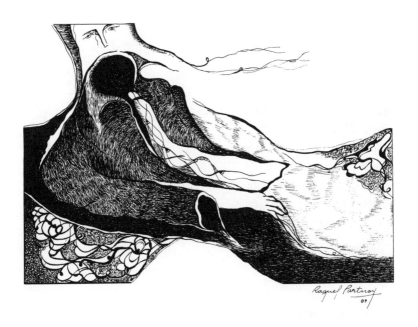

Cuatro postales

I.

La muerte, mi vecina,
lo convenció a mi hermano
de que tomara
unas vacaciones de la vida.
Y él, una mañana,
apagó la luz con el gatillo.
En donde está no hay postales
para mandar a los amigos ...

II.

La muerte, mi vecina,
me golpeó la puerta un mediodía;
venía a pedirme
"una tacita de arrepentimiento"
y una pizca
"sólo una pizca" de cobardía.
"Vuelva mañana" le dije.
Y esa noche me mudé.

III.

La muerte, mi vecina,
me descubrió una tarde
con los ojos vendados,
cubierta de frazadas
que olían
a cuerpos sucios y aterrados.

Four Postcards

I.

Death, my neighbor,
convinced my brother
that he should
take a vacation from life.
And he, one morning,
put out the light with the trigger.
Where he is there are no postcards
to send home to friends . . .

II.

Death, my neighbor,
knocked hard on my door one day at noontime;
she wanted to borrow
"a cup of repentance"
and a pinch
"just a pinch" of cowardice.
"Come back tomorrow," I told her.
That night I moved away.

III.

Death, my neighbor,
found me one afternoon
blindfolded,
wrapped in blankets
that reeked
of filthy and terrified bodies.

No la ahuyentó el olor, estoy segura,
porque ese mismo día
llevó a ZulmaMaríaElenaBenjayBraco
que portaban idénticas frazadas.
La muerte calzaba botas militares.

IV.

La muerte, mi vecina,
harta ya de que la ande esquivando,
vendrá descalza un día
a llevarse mis huesos
a un país de lluvias sin futuro.
¡Ojalá que se ahogue en mis cenizas!

The stench didn't scare her away, though, I'm sure,
because that same day,
she took away ZulmaMaríaElenaBenjaandBraco
who were wrapped in identical blankets.
Death was wearing military boots.

IV.

Death, my neighbor,
fed up with me for giving her the slip,
will one day come, barefoot,
to carry off my bones
to a country of rain that has no future.
Oh I hope she chokes on my ashes!

Relato (A mi hermano)

Con un miedo delgado
me aventuré en tu vida
muchos años atrás
cuando el sol era nuevo,
las manzanas buscaban
tus dientes, decididas,
y el río de limones
no te había emboscado.
Yo, que andaba muy lejos,
vivía de prestado,
y me sentía hermana
del viento y la locura,
descifrando señales
fui perdiendo la huella.
Despué, ya fue muy tarde:
te habías suicidado.

A Tale (For My Brother)

Carrying a sliver of fear,
I ventured into your life
many years ago
when the sun was new,
when the apples, determined,
sought out your teeth,
when the river of lemons
had not yet ambushed you.
And I, who journeyed far off,
living on borrowed time,
felt I was a sister
to madness and the wind:
deciphering signs
I strayed from your trail.
Afterwards, it was too late:
you had taken your own life.

Epitafio

De todas las libertades
tal vez
elegiste la muerte.

Y las acuarelas de nuestra infancia
se van
deshaciendo en el humo.

Por los salitrales te buscaré
cuando el sol me deje mirar atras.

Llegaré a tu tumba para dejarte
un gajo de almendro
y un poema muerto
de angustia que vos
ya ilustraste con sangre.

Epitaph

Of all the freedoms
you, perhaps,
chose death.

And the watercolors of our childhood
are fading
vanishing into thin air ...

Through the salt marsh I will search for you
when the sun allows me to look back.

I will arrive at your grave to leave you
a branch broken off an almond tree,
and a poem killed by anguish, which you
have already illustrated with your blood.

Razones

El viento del salitral
agrió el vino de tus sueños
te sacudió los andamios
de construir el futuro
después te enredó los dedos
contra el filo de un gatillo.
Fué una mentira de plomo,
fué una avalancha de sal,
fué el viento, mi hermano, el viento,
infierno del salitral.

The Reasons Why

The wind in the salt marsh
soured the wine of your dreams,
shook the scaffolding
on which you were building the future,
then it pressed your finger
against the trigger's edge.
It was a lie made of lead,
it was an avalanche of salt,
it was the wind, my brother, the wind.
Hell in the salt marsh.

Compañero de juegos

Jugamos con las sombras
por detrás de las puertas,
jugamos con la escarcha,
con las ramas desnudas.
Jugamos con las piedras,
con las cosas perdidas
en el patio de casa.

Cuando llegó el momento
nos jugamos la vida.

Yo me gané una celda
y me gané el destierro,
y unos cuantos suspiros
ante el deber cumplido.
Vos perdiste sonrisas,
perdiste la inocencia
y ganaste la paz
debajo de la tierra

hoy las sombras no juegan
y la escarcha se extiende
sobre ramas desnudas
piedras del cementerio
pregunto dónde fueron
esas cosas perdidas.

Yo me he quedado sola
jugando con la vida . . .

Playmate

We played with the shadows
behind our door,
we played with the frost,
with the naked branches.
We played with the stones,
with things lost
in the yard of our home.

And when the time came
we played at life.

My prize was a jail cell
and exile,
and two or three sighs
for fulfilling my duty.
You lost your smile,
your innocence,
and your prize was peace
under the earth.

Today the shadows no longer play
and the frost spreads
over the naked branches,
the gravestones.
I ask myself what has become
of the things we lost.

I am left here, alone,
playing with my life . . .

Confesión

... A falta de otros bienes
llevo a cuestas mis más viejos poemas.
Ellos suplen las cosas
y las gentes
que me arrancó la lucha despareja.
Maltrechos y arrugados,
yo los aliso sobre las hojas nuevas ...
y vienen a contarme unas historias
que no tienen siquiera moraleja.
Hoy quiero confesarte, amigo mío,
que ya no soy poeta:
soy embalsamadora de poesías.
A falta de otros bienes
ando con mis cadáveres a cuestas.

Confession

... As I have no other belongings
I carry my oldest poems over my back.
They make up for the things,
for the people,
that an uneven struggle took from me.
Torn, wrinkled,
I smooth them out on new sheets of paper ...
and they come to tell me stories
that don't even have a moral.
Today I want to confess to you, my friend,
I am no longer a poet:
I am an embalmer of poetry.
As I have no other belongings,
I am walking with my corpses over my back.

Arte Poética

Eso que vuela bajito
es mi poesía.
Rastreadora de olores
dentro del pasto.
Yo no busco la altura.
Vértigo el vuelo.
Embisto la distancia
volando bajo.
Allí está la palabra,
olvidadita,
fresca con las raíces
u oliendo a miedo.
Tornasoleándose algo
como la carne
cadáver que transita
a la semilla.

Ars Poetica

That which flies close to the ground
is my poetry.
Tracker of scents
among the weeds.
I do not seek lofty heights.
Heights make me dizzy.
So I charge down on distance,
flying low.
There lies the word:
sweet, forgotten,
fresh with the roots
or smelling of fear.
And it is opalescent
like the flesh
of a human corpse going
to seed.

IV.
Testimonies
Testimonios

Venganza de la manzana

Me arrojaron
como piedra,
yuyo, yerba mala;
separada,
la manzana podrida,
subversiva . . .
Pero ahora
fermentan
las manzanas
restantes,
es decir,
vienen fermentando
desde antes
de que a mí
me sacaron del cajón.

Pero ahora
caterva de milicos
y oligarcas,
prepárense
para morir borrachos,
empachados,
incurablemente intoxicados,
sumergidos
hasta las orejas
en el dulce jugo
de la Gran Sidra Nacional.

Revenge of the Apple

They tossed me away
like a stone,
a weed, an evil herb;
separated out
the rotten, subversive
apple . . .
And now
all the rest of
the apples
are fermenting;
in fact,
they have been fermenting
since before
they tossed me from
the crate.

And now
horde of oligarchs
and generals:
prepare to die drunk,
nauseated,
incurably intoxicated,
sunk
up to your ears
in the sweet juice
of the Great National Cider.

Tragedia para dos voces, un coro y un país

Coro

No me hablen de las puertas del infierno.
Yo estuve allí, pero antes fue la vida.
Marchaba mi esperanza por las calles,
giraba el nuevo día en mi reloj,
en mi garganta el grito que transforma,
en mis manos la semilla o la cruz.
Supo mi sol estallar también de ira
ante lo injusto. Peligroso mi sol.
Vinieron a arrestarme, era la noche
de mi nación, la noche de su historia.
No entendieron razones ni buscaron
más que horadarme la carne y la conciencia.
No me hablen de las puertas del infierno,
yo estuve allí, tierra de la tortura.
Me envolví en mi bandera y tuve frío.
Me envolví en mi bandera
de ideales.

La voz de la madre

Yo conjuré a las piedras
en nombre de mi hijo.
La piedras se partieron
pero no lo encontré.

Yo conjuré al silencio
en nombre de mi hijo,
y se pobló de quejas
pero él no me habló.

Tragedy for Two Voices,
a Chorus and a Country

Chorus

Do not speak to me of Hell's Gates.
I was there. But before, was life.
My hope marched down the streets,
the new day circled round my watch,
in my throat the shout that transformed,
in my hands the seed or the cross.
My sun knew how to explode with rage
before injustice. My sun, my dangerous sun.
They came to arrest me, it was a sinister time
for the nation, a sinister time for History.
They refused to listen to reason's voice,
they only wanted to pierce my flesh, my conscience.
Do not speak to me of Hell's Gates.
I was there, a land of torture.
I wrapped myself in my flag and I was cold.
I wrapped myself in my flag
of ideals.

The Mother's Voice

I conjured up the stones
in the name of my son.
The stones split open
but I did not find him.

I conjured up the silence
in the name of my son,
and it filled with groans
but I did not hear him.

Yo conjuré a los hombres
en nombre de mi hijo.
Los hombres se alinearon
para su ejecución.

Coro

... Y no nombré más nombres que mi nombre.
O tal vez les conté de mis amigos ...
Quién sabe si en las trampas de la muerte
quise cambiar entrega por alivio.
No me sentía ni traidor ni héroe,
fuí solamente un desaparecido.
No me hablen de las puertas del infierno.
Mi bandera hecha harapos, tuve frío ...

La voz de un hombre

Vengo de donde
muchos no vuelven.
Sobreviviente.
Abro mi boca
y habla su voz
sobreviviente.
Yo llevo en ristre
su estandarte
sobreviviente.
Y a veces lloro
de rabia y miedo
sobreviviendo.

I conjured up humankind
in the name of my son
and humankind lined up
for his execution.

Chorus

... And I named no names but my own name.
Or maybe I did tell them about my friends ...
Who knows whether, in Death's trap,
I tried to exchange submission for relief.
I felt I was neither a traitor nor a hero,
I was just one *desaparecido.*
Do not speak to me of Hell's Gates:
My flag was in tatters, I was so cold ...

The Voice of a Man

From whence I come
many do not return.
A survivor.
I open my mouth
and their voice speaks.
A survivor.
I carry their flag
at the ready.
A survivor.
And at times I weep
filled with rage and fear
surviving.

La voz de la madre

... Y me cubrí las canas
con un pañuelo blanco.
Y me fuí con las madres
de todos, a marchar.
Mi dolor era un zonda
viento, que purifica
arrasando a los tibios.
Fuí un arma mi dolor.

Coro

Yo anduve el país de los cadalsos,
de mano en mano y con mi sangre a cuestas;
y ahora que mi historia se dibuja
de boca en boca y callan los culpables,
mis huesos van reclamando justicia
de puerta en puerta
y aunque ya sea tarde.

The Mother's Voice

... And I covered my grey hair
with a white kerchief.
And I went with all
the mothers, to march.
My pain was a scorching hot
and purifying north wind,
sweeping away the indifferent.
My pain was my weapon.

Chorus

I passed through a country of Death's scaffolds,
thrown from hand to hand, my blood over my back;
and now that my story is being told
from mouth to mouth and the guilty keep silent,
my bones go demanding justice
from door to door
even though it is now late.

El mensaje

Me piden el mensaje
como una piedra
fundamental
como una salvación.

El mensaje.

Yo sólo traigo
el hecho
como el cartero
el sobre:
gritos
tortura
esa injusticia grande.
Las raíces
sin agua
los
desaparecidos.

El mensaje,

si de verdad
lo invocan,
caerá
como una catarata amarga
sobre sus vientres.
Luego echarán a andar
o quedarán
clavados en sí mismos
esperando
el Mensaje.

My Message

They ask me for my message
as though it were a
cornerstone
or offered some kind of salvation.

My message.

Like the postman,
like envelopes,
I bring only
facts:
screams
torture
that great injustice,
roots
without water
the
disappeared.

My message,

if they truly
insist on it,
will pour down
like a bitter waterfall
on their bellies.
Then they will either take off walking
or stay
rooted in themselves
waiting
for my Message.

A Rodrigo Rojas

*Cuando a los diecinueve años los militares chilenos lo
quemaron vivo, empapelamos las calles del barrio con
afiches con su foto, llamando a la manifestación.*

Desde los postes Rodrigo nos saluda
y desde las paradas
de los autobuses.
Te reirías tanto, compañero,
si te contáramos que en todas las fotos
tenés cara de santo, tanto
te reirías.

Desde la muerte tu risa nos saluda
y va endulzando la acidez del duelo
con la dulzura de la sangre joven
que nos refresca la raíz del odio.

Desde el futuro tu vida nos saluda
y amartillamos sin piedad nuestras conciencias
que ya es la hora de cobrárnoslo todo:
la sal en las heridas, tu muerte y el incendio
del corazón del alba y la inocencia.

To Rodrigo Rojas

When, at nineteen, he was burned alived by the Chilean military, we covered the streets of El Barrio with posters of Rodrigo Rojas' picture, calling people to a demonstration.

From the lampposts Rodrigo greets us
as well as from the bus stops.
You'd die laughing, *compañero*,
if we told you how in all these photos
you look just like a saint, oh!, how
you'd die laughing.

From Death your laughter greets us
and sweetens the acid taste of our grief
with the sweetness of your youthful blood
watering the roots of our hatred.

From the Future your life greets us
and mercilessly we cock the trigger of conscience
for it is time to collect all that is owed us:
the salt in our wounds, your death, the burning
heart of dawn, and the innocence.

Juicio

Aquí
mis muertos tienen
que probar que sus muertes se debieron
a "circunstancias extremas y aberrantes."

A mí se me ha exigido una evidencia
de que no fué mi voluntad la de esfumarme
entre enero y abril, hace diez años.

Cómo consigo pruebas convincentes
de aquel que se tragó el miedo caliente
y le arden la laringe y el esófago
la punta de la lengua y las verdades?

Bahía Blanca, Semana Santa de 1987

Judgment

Here
my dead must prove
their deaths were due to
"extreme and aberrant circumstances."

I am required to provide evidence
that I did not vanish of my own free will
from January to April, ten years ago.

How can I get convincing evidence
from that one who swallowed burning fear
and scalded his larynx, his esophagus,
the tip of his tongue and the truth?

Bahía Blanca, Argentina, Easter Week of 1987

Testimonio de
Robert Duval de Haití

I.

... *en esa piecita*
(Robert Duval cuenta)
ciento ochenta
vi morir enfrente mío.

Doscientos cincuenta
escuchamos.

II.

... *en esa piecita*
a veces treinta
o cuarenta
según
los que habían mandado a morir
aquel día ...
un bowl nos daban
con comida
caliente la volcábamos en el piso
el mismo
con agua.
Había que tomarla
allí mismo
porque
el mismo
bowl para la otra celda
y la otra
todas.

Testimony of
Robert Duval from Haiti

I.

... in that tiny room
(Robert Duval recounts)
I saw one hundred and eighty
die in front of me.

Two hundred and fifty of us
are listening.

II.

... in that tiny room
sometimes thirty
or forty,
depending on how many
had been sent to die
that day ...
They gave us a bowl
of hot food
that we had to empty on the ground
because this same bowl
was for the water
that we had to drink down
right then
because
this same bowl
was for the next cell,
for the others,
all the others.

III.

dice:
enfrentar el sistema
nos costó
diez muertos
en cada manifestación.
Invertimos sangre.
dice:
todavia no vimos
la tumba colectiva.
Estamos por verla.

IV.

dice:
yo denuncié
denuncié
denuncié.
Entonces dice:
hay que reflexionar profundamente
sobre la conducta
represiva.

III.

He says:
confronting the system
cost us
ten dead
at each demonstration.
We sacrificed blood.
He says:
still we have not seen
the mass grave.
But we are about to see it.

IV.

He says:
I denounced
I denounced
I denounced.
Then he says:
we have to think long and hard
about repressive behavior.

Testimonio de
Sonia de El Salvador

1 desaparecida
2 asesinados
5 encarceladas
10 exilados
de los 20
que estudiábamos allí.
Yo
no estaba organizada.
Todavía.

Testimony of
Sonia from El Salvador

Of the 20
of us who were studying there:
1 disappeared
2 assassinated
5 imprisoned
10 exiled.
I
was not involved.
Yet.

Testimonio de
Lucía Ramírez de El Salvador

Nosotros
los damnificados
los desplazados
los marginados
miles
y miles.
Lejos
de que nos dejen
organizar.
Lejos.
Capturas de muchos
compañeros.
Marta Lidia Guzmán
desaparecida.
El cuatro de julio.
Incluyendo
pues
mi persona
capturados.
Esta es la respuesta que el gobierno nos ha dado en lugar de la
ayuda internacional que nos habían enviado solidariamente
a
nosotros
los
damnificados.
aburridos
de tanta masacre.

Testimony of
Lucía Ramírez from El Salvador

We
the victims
the displaced
the marginalized
thousands
upon thousands.
So far
from allowing us
to organize.
So far.
So many compañeros
captured.
Marta Lidia Guzmán
disappeared.
On the Fourth of July.
Even
I
myself
captured.
This is what we received from the government instead of the
international help which had been sent to us in solidarity
to
us
the
victims
sick and tired
of so much carnage.

Canción de la exiliada

Me cortaron la voz:
dos voces tengo.
En dos lenguas distintas
mi canto vierto.
Me arrancaron el sol:
dos soles nuevos
como dos relucientes
tambores sueno.
Me aislaron de mi gente
y hoy a mi pueblo
vuelve mi canto doble
como en un eco.
Y a pesar de lo obscuro
de este destierro,
se enciende hoy mi poesía
contra un espejo.
Me cortaron la voz,
dos voces tengo.

Song of the Exiled

They cut out my voice:
I have two voices.
I pour out my songs
in two different tongues.
They stripped me of the sun:
two new suns
like two resplendent drums
I am playing.
They isolated me from my people
and today my twin song
is returning like an echo
to my people. And
in spite of the darkness
of this banishment,
today my poetry is aflame
before the mirror.
They cut out my voice:
I have two voices.

Testimonio

El micrófono
me hace una reverencia
de cables enroscados.
Yo a mi vez me le acerco
abro los ojos,
abro
el libro,
abro
la boca.
Eso sí, abro bastante la boca
y ahí les cuento.
Dicen
que hablo muy suave
que casi les murmuro
que no oyen
los gritos perforantes.
Yo abro
el recuerdo
como un melón podrido.

Dicen
que no consigo
describir con rigor las inclemencias
de la picana.
Dicen que en estas cosas
no debe quedar ningún espacio
librado
a la imaginación o a la duda.
Saco
el informe de Amnistía
y hablo por esa tinta.
Digo: "Lean."
Yo a mi vez me enrosco

Testimony

This microphone
with its cable coiling around it,
bows to me.
I walk up to it,
open my eyes
open
my book
open
my mouth.
That's right, I open my mouth wide
and begin my story.
They say
I speak too softly,
that I am practically mumbling,
that they can't hear
the screams piercing.
I open
my memory
like a rotten cantaloupe.

They say
I have not managed
to forcefully convey the pitiless rage
of the cattle prod.
They say that in matters such as this
nothing must be left
open
to the imagination or to doubt.
I take out
the Amnesty report
and begin speaking through that ink.
I urge: "Read."
I, in my turn, coil around

en la reverencia cómplice
del micrófono.
Enarbolo la acción como receta,
la información como antídoto infalible
y, una vez desatado cada nudo,
digo mis versos.
Resistí. Voy entera.

my bowing accomplice,
this microphone.
I urge action as a prescription,
information as an infallible antidote
and, once every knot is untied,
I recite my verses.
I resist. I am whole.

About the Author

Alicia Partnoy was born in Argentina in 1955. During her years as a political prisoner her stories and poems were smuggled out of prison and published anonymously in human rights journals. Since her arrival in the United States, she has lectured extensively at the invitation of Amnesty International, universities and community groups. Alicia has presented testimony on human rights violations to the United Nations, the Organization of American States, Amnesty International, and human rights organizations in Argentina. Her testimony is quoted in *Nunca Más: The Final Report of the Argentine Commission for the Investigation of Disappearance*. She is best known as the author of *The Little School: Tales of Disappearance and Survival in Argentina* (Cleis Press, 1986). Alicia Partnoy also edited *You Can't Drown the Fire: Latin American Women Writing in Exile* (Cleis Press, 1988). *Revenge of the Apple* is her first collection of poetry. Alicia Partnoy has two daughters, Ruth, whose stories she tells in her tales of imprisonment and exile, and Eva Victoria, born in the United States. She is a member of the board of directors of Amnesty International U.S.A. She lives with her husband in Washington D.C.

Books from Cleis Press

Latin American Studies

Beyond the Border: A New Age in Latin American Women's Fiction edited by Nora Erro-Peralta and Caridad Silva-Núñez. ISBN: 0-939416-42-5 24.95 cloth; ISBN: 0-939416-43-3 12.95 paper.

The Little School: Tales of Disappearance and Survival in Argentina by Alicia Partnoy. ISBN: 0-939416-08-5 21.95 cloth; ISBN: 0-939416-07-7 9.95 paper.

You Can't Drown the Fire: Latin American Women Writing in Exile edited by Alicia Partnoy. ISBN: 0-939416-16-6 24.95 cloth; ISBN: 0-939416-17-4 9.95 paper.

Women's Studies

Peggy Deery: An Irish Family at War by Nell McCafferty. ISBN: 0-939416-38-7 24.95 cloth; ISBN: 0-939416-39-5 9.95 paper.

The Shape of Red: Insider/Outsider Reflections by Ruth Hubbard and Margaret Randall. ISBN: 0-939416-19-0 24.95 cloth; ISBN: 0-939416-18-2 9.95 paper.

Women & Honor: Some Notes on Lying by Adrienne Rich. ISBN: 0-939416-44-1 3.95 paper.

Fiction

Another Love by Erzsébet Galgóczi. ISBN: 0-939416-52-2 24.95 cloth; ISBN: 0-939416-51-4 8.95 paper.

Cosmopolis: Urban Stories by Women edited by Ines Rieder. ISBN: 0-939416-36-0 24.95 cloth; ISBN: 0-939416-37-9 9.95 paper.

Night Train To Mother by Ronit Lentin. ISBN: 0-939416-29-8 24.95 cloth; ISBN: 0-939416-28-X 9.95 paper.

The One You Call Sister: New Women's Fiction edited by Paula Martinac. ISBN: 0-939416-30-1 24.95 cloth; ISBN: 0-939416031-X 9.95 paper.

Unholy Alliances: New Women's Fiction edited by Louise Rafkin. ISBN: 0-939416-14-X 21.95 cloth; ISBN: 0-939416-15-8 9.95 paper.

The Wall by Marlen Haushofer. ISBN: 0-939416-53-0 24.95 cloth; ISBN: 0-939416-54-9 paper.

Health/Recovery Titles:

The Absence of the Dead Is Their Way of Appearing by Mary Winfrey Trautmann. ISBN: 0-939416-04-2 8.95 paper.

AIDS: The Women edited by Ines Rieder and Patricia Ruppelt.
ISBN: 0-939416-20-4 24.95 cloth; ISBN: 0-939416-21-2 9.95 paper.

Don't: A Woman's Word by Elly Danica. ISBN: 0-939416-23-9 21.95 cloth;
ISBN: 0-939416-22-0 8.95 paper.

1 in 3: Women with Cancer Confront an Epidemic edited by Judith Brady.
ISBN: 0-939416-50-6 24.95 cloth; ISBN: 0-939416-49-2 10.95 paper.

Voices in the Night: Women Speaking About Incest edited by Toni A.H.
McNaron and Yarrow Morgan. ISBN: 0-939416-02-6 9.95 paper.

With the Power of Each Breath: A Disabled Women's Anthology edited by
Susan Browne, Debra Connors and Nanci Stern. ISBN: 0-939416-09-3 24.95
cloth; ISBN: 0-939416-06-9 10.95 paper.

Woman-Centered Pregnancy and Birth by the Federation of Feminist
Women's Health Centers. ISBN: 0-939416-03-4 11.95 paper.

Animal Rights

*And a Deer's Ear, Eagle's Song and Bear's Grace: Relationships Between
Animals and Women* edited by Theresa Corrigan and Stephanie T. Hoppe.
ISBN: 0-939416-38-7 24.95 cloth; ISBN: 0-939416-39-5 9.95 paper.

*With a Fly's Eye, Whale's Wit and Woman's Heart: Relationships Between
Animals and Women* edited by Theresa Corrigan and Stephanie T. Hoppe.
ISBN: 0-939416-24-7 24.95 cloth; ISBN: 0-939416-25-5 9.95 paper.

Sexuality/Lesbian Studies

A Lesbian Love Advisor by Celeste West. ISBN: 0-939416-27-1 24.95 cloth;
ISBN: 0-939416-26-3 9.95 paper.

Boomer: Railroad Memoirs by Linda Niemann. ISBN: 0-939416-55-7
12.95 paper.

Different Daughters: A Book by Mothers of Lesbians edited by Louise Rafkin.
ISBN: 0-939416-12-3 21.95 cloth; ISBN: 0-939416-13-1 9.95 paper.

Different Mothers: Sons & Daughters of Lesbians Talk About Their Lives
edited by Louise Rafkin. ISBN: 0-939416-40-9 24.95 cloth;
ISBN: 0-939416-41-7 9.95 paper.

Good Sex: Real Stories From Real People by Julia Hutton.
ISBN: 0-939416-56-5 24.95 cloth; ISBN: 0-939416-57-3 12.95 paper.

Long Way Home: The Odyssey of a Lesbian Mother and Her Children by
Jeanne Jullion. ISBN: 0-939416-05-0 8.95 paper.

More Serious Pleasure: Lesbian Erotic Stories and Poetry edited by the
Sheba Collective. ISBN: 0-939416-48-4 24.95 cloth; ISBN: 0-939416-47-6
9.95 paper.

Serious Pleasure: Lesbian Erotic Stories and Poetry edited by the Sheba Collective. ISBN: 0-939416-46-8 24.95 cloth; ISBN: 0-939416-45-X 9.95 paper.

Sex Work: Writings by Women in the Sex Industry edited by Frédérique Delacoste and Priscilla Alexander. ISBN: 0-939416-10-7 24.95 cloth; ISBN: 0-939416-11-5 16.95 paper.

Susie Bright's Sexual Reality: A Virtual Sex World Reader. ISBN: 0-939416-58-1 24.95 cloth; ISBN: 0-939416-59-X 9.95 paper

Susie Sexpert's Lesbian Sex World by Susie Bright. ISBN: 0-939416-34-4 24.95 cloth; ISBN: 0-939416-35-2 9.95 paper.

Since 1980, Cleis Press has published progressive books by women. We welcome your order and will ship your books as quickly as possible. Individual orders must be prepaid (U.S. dollars only). Please add 15% shipping. PA residents add 6% sales tax. Mail orders: Cleis Press, PO Box 8933, Pittsburgh PA 15221. MasterCard and Visa orders: $25 minimum—include account number, exp. date, and signature. FAX your credit card order: (412) 937-1567. Or, phone us Mon-Fri, 9 am - 5 pm EST: (412) 937-1555.